ESSENTIAL TIPS

101

PRESERVING FRUIT

D0732328

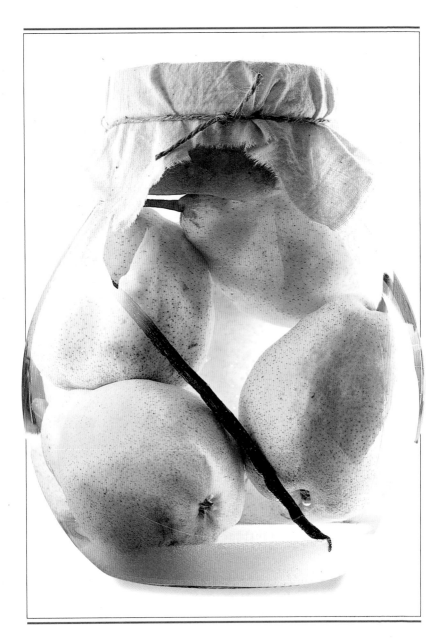

ESSENTIAL **101** TIPS

PRESERVING FRUIT

Oded Schwartz

Food styling by Oded Schwartz

DK PUBLISHING, INC.

A DK PUBLISHING BOOK

Editor Simon Adams
Art Editor Alison Shackleton
Senior Editor Gillian Roberts
Series Art Editor Alison Donovan
Production Controller Jenny May
US Editor Ray Rogers

**Follow either imperial or metric units throughout a recipe,
never a mixture of the two, since they are not exact equivalents.**

First American Edition, 1998
2 4 6 8 10 9 7 5 3
Published in the United States by DK Publishing, Inc.
95 Madison Avenue, New York, New York 10016

Visit us on the World Wide Web at http://www.dk.com

ISBN 0-7894-2779-6

Text film output by R&B Creative Services Ltd, Great Britain
Reproduced by Colourscan, Singapore
Printed and bound in Italy by Graphicom

ESSENTIAL TIPS

PAGES 26–37

JAMS & PRESERVES

PAGES 38–42

JELLIES

PAGES 43–47

FRUIT IN SYRUP OR ALCOHOL

PAGES 48–53

BUTTERS, CURDS, & CHEESES

INGREDIENTS

1 WHY PRESERVE?

The ancient technique of preserving fruit adds a distinctive and delicious flavor to fresh produce. Preserving large quantities of seasonal fruit spreads the enjoyment of the fruit throughout the year, providing a larder of jams, jellies, and preserves to be used in all forms of cooking.

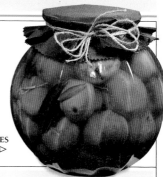

CLEMENTINES IN BRANDY ▷

2 THE PRESERVING YEAR

Through summer and autumn, soft and orchard fruits are in season and therefore usually cheapest and best: these are the seasons in which to preserve fruit as jellies, syrups, jams, and whole-fruit conserves. In winter, citrus fruit come into their own, for making marmalade, while spring is the ideal time to prepare for the preserving year ahead.

3 SOFT FRUIT

Soft fruit are high in pectin and acid, and make wonderful jams, jellies, and preserves. Choose firm, unblemished fruit with no bruises or mold. Use as soon as possible: soft fruit do not keep.

REDCURRANTS ▷

WHITE-CURRANTS ▷

△ BLACKBERRIES

△ BLUEBERRIES

△ RASPBERRIES

STRAWBERRIES ▷

△ BLACKCURRANTS

△ GOOSEBERRIES

4 ORCHARD FRUIT

Most orchard fruit, especially apples, are high in pectin (needed for set), so play an important role in jam- and jelly-making. Although you can use apples on their own, they lose their flavor in cooking and are mainly added to boost the pectin content of other fruit.

△ DAMSONS

△ CRAB-APPLES

△ APRICOT

MONTMORENCY △ CHERRIES

BLACK CHERRIES ▷

△ GREENGAGE

△ SUNGOLD PLUM

△ SWITZEN PLUM

◁ YELLOW PEACH

WHITE PEACH ▷

△ PACKHAM PEAR

△ WILLIAMS PEAR

△ GRANNY SMITH APPLE

◁ BRAMLEY APPLE

QUINCE ▷

9

5 CITRUS FRUIT

Citrus fruit make delicious conserves and marmalades. They also play an essential role in preserving other kinds of fruit since they are rich in pectin and acid, and achieve a good set when added to jams and jellies. Do not discard the seeds, since they contain the highest amount of pectin: tie them in a piece of muslin and add to the boiling fruit. Citrus fruit are also a good source of vitamin C, which prevents fruit from discoloring. Citrus fruit may have a wax coating: scrub in hot water to remove it.

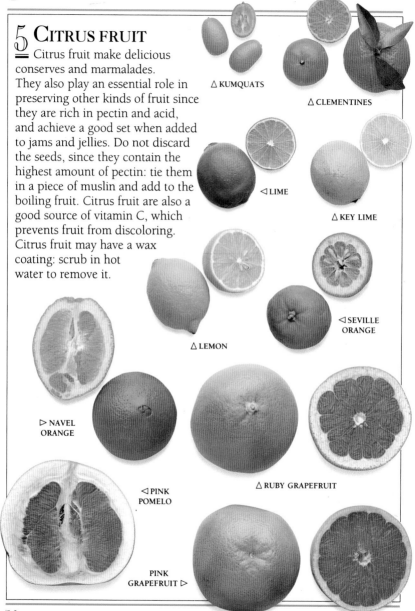

△ KUMQUATS

△ CLEMENTINES

◁ LIME

△ KEY LIME

◁ SEVILLE ORANGE

△ LEMON

▷ NAVEL ORANGE

△ RUBY GRAPEFRUIT

◁ PINK POMELO

PINK GRAPEFRUIT ▷

6 EXOTIC FRUIT

There is no precise definition of an exotic fruit – what is rare in one part of the world is common in another. Most exotic fruit have evocative aromas and vibrant colors that enhance and flavor other foods. They also make wonderful preserves. Buy the freshest produce possible with a good fragrance and no signs of bruising. Store in a cool, dark place; use quickly while still at their best.

△ LITCHIS

△ PASSION FRUIT

△ FRESH FIG

△ FRESH DATES

△ KIWI FRUIT

△ GUAVA

△ PERSIMMONS

△ PRICKLY PEARS

△ MANGOES

△ POMEGRANATE

FINGER BANANAS ▷

△ PINEAPPLE

△ RED BANANAS

11

7 SPICES & HERBS

Spices and herbs add flavor to a preserve and help the preserving process. Ground spices quickly lose their aroma, so grind whole ones just before use. Store fresh herbs in a cool place. The flavor of some dried herbs is more concentrated than fresh, so use half the quantity.

8 SUGAR PRESERVATIVES

Many kinds of sugar are now available; most are inter-changeable. White refined sugars produce a clear, hard-set preserve; honey and raw sugars give a softer product.

▷ GRANULATED &
PRESERVING SUGARS
These two refined sugars are inter-changeable; preserving sugar is rarely available.

△ GRANULATED
SUGAR

△ PRESERVING
SUGAR

△ RAW SUGAR
A mild-flavored sugar, refined or unrefined.

△ LIGHT BROWN SUGAR
Containing molasses, this is a raw, all-purpose sugar.

△ DARK BROWN SUGAR
Moist and dark, with a pronounced depth of sugary flavor.

△ MOLASSES SUGAR
Soft and very moist, this sugar has a strong flavor.

△ JAGGERY
This raw Indian sugar has a distinct flavor.

▷ LIQUID
GLUCOSE
This complex sugar helps prevent crystallization.

▷ PALM SUGAR
A fragrant and tasty syrup from the sap of palms.

◁ HONEY
Use single-flower honey for distinct flavor.

▷ MOLASSES
A richly flavored by-product of sugar refining.

9 ACID PRESERVATIVES

Acids are very important, since they help jams and jellies to set and prevent discoloration. To retain their freshness, buy in small quantities and keep in airtight containers.

▷ TAMARIND
This sweet-sour acid is the pulp of the tamarind pod.

△ LEMON JUICE
A natural antioxidant, lemon juice adds pectin and enhances color.

△ VITAMIN C
An antioxidant, vitamin C helps to preserve a good color.

△ CITRIC ACID
Sometimes sold as lemon salt, citric acid can be used in place of lemon juice.

10 VINEGAR PRESERVATIVES

Select clear vinegars with a good color and aroma. White and pale vinegars, such as cider, white wine, or rice vinegar, are used for pickles. Dark vinegars, such as red wine and malt, are suitable for chutneys and flavoring.

CIDER   WHITE WINE

RED WINE   MALT

11 ALCOHOL PRESERVATIVES

Pure alcohol is the ideal preservative, since bacteria cannot grow in it. It can be used on its own or mixed with a heavy syrup.

You can use just about any kind of spirit for preserving – rum, brandy, and eau de vie are ideal – but make sure it is no less than 80 proof.

BASIC EQUIPMENT

12 KITCHEN ESSENTIALS

You will need a variety of good-quality kitchen equipment for successful and efficient preserving. Sharp knives are essential, as are ladles, skimmers, and wooden spoons. Use glass, china, or stainless-steel items; avoid reactive metals such as aluminum. However, do not use a metal sieve with acidic fruit since the metal can affect both the color and flavor of the finished preserve.

▷ STAINLESS-STEEL BOWL

△ GLASS MIXING BOWLS

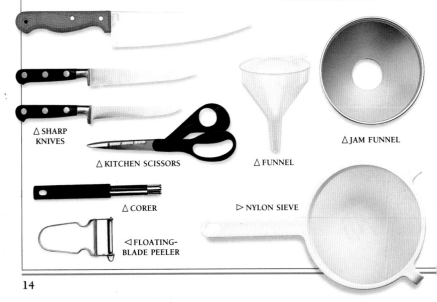

△ SHARP KNIVES

△ KITCHEN SCISSORS

△ FUNNEL

△ JAM FUNNEL

△ CORER

▷ NYLON SIEVE

◁ FLOATING-BLADE PEELER

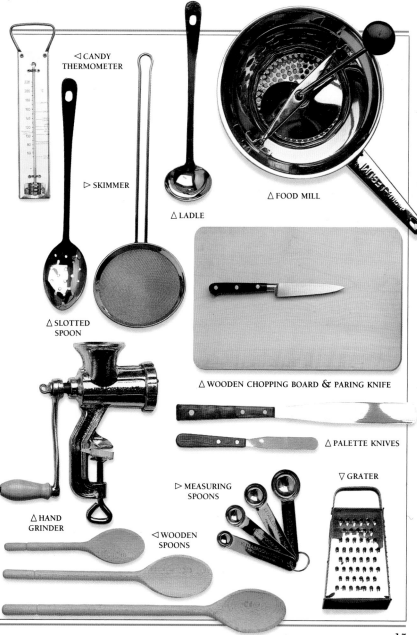

◁ CANDY THERMOMETER

▷ SKIMMER

◁ LADLE

△ FOOD MILL

△ SLOTTED SPOON

△ WOODEN CHOPPING BOARD & PARING KNIFE

△ PALETTE KNIVES

▽ GRATER

△ HAND GRINDER

▷ MEASURING SPOONS

◁ WOODEN SPOONS

15

FILTER MATERIALS
Calico (top), muslin (center), and filter papers (bottom) are used to strain fruit.

13 FILTERS & BAGS

Avoid artificial materials; use natural ones – such as unbleached muslin, cheesecloth, or calico – for filtering and straining fruit. Natural, unbleached materials will not affect the taste or quality of the preserve. To make successful jellies, you will need a muslin jelly bag (*Tip 33*). Before you use any of these natural materials, sterilize them by pouring boiling water through them. Allow to dry before use. To filter small quantities of liquid, use commercial, readily available coffee filter papers.

14 PRESERVING PANS

The choice of pan depends on the preserve you are making. Use a wide, narrow-bottomed copper pan to make non-acidic jams and jellies, and a stainless-steel pan to make chutneys and pickles, which have a high concentration of acid. Keep all pans scrupulously clean.

△ **NON-CORROSIVE PRESERVING PAN**
The thick, heavy base of a stainless-steel pan prevents hot spots and protects the preserve from burning.

◁ **COPPER PRESERVING PAN**
Use a copper preserving pan with a capacity of about 16 pints (9 liters).

15 THE RIGHT JAR

Glass is the ideal material to show off preserves at their best, and is also non-corrosive. Reused glass jars are only really suitable for short-term storage. For long-term storage and preservation, use new preserving jars that are suited to high temperatures and have non-corrosive seals and rings.

ALL SIZES & SHAPES OF GLASS JAR

16 JARS WITHOUT LIDS

For a preserve with high sugar content or acidity, store in a lidless jar sealed with both a waxed paper disk and cellophane seal. However, if you want to keep it longer than 3 months, heat-process in a lidded jar (*Tip 24*).

17 JARS WITH LIDS

If your preserve is to be heat-processed, use a specialized preserving jar with lid. Select whatever kind is most readily available and for which spare new lids or rubber seals can easily be bought. It is always advisable to use new jars that have acid-resistant seals. With one-piece lidded jars, you can see when a vacuum has formed and also if the seal is broken. (Bottles without lids require corks to seal them: always use new corks.)

Seal & clamp-top jar lid

One-piece lid

Screw-band seal & lid

△ CLAMP-TOP JAR   △ VACUUM ONE-PIECE LIDDED JAR   △ VACUUM LID & SCREW-BAND JAR

TECHNIQUES

18 STERILIZING JARS

All glass jars must be sterilized before use. Place the washed jars in a deep pan, cover with boiling water, and boil rapidly for 10 minutes. Drain the jars on a kitchen towel and dry in a cool oven. Lids, seals, and corks must be immersed in boiling water for a few seconds. To sterilize in the oven, place jars on a tray in a preheated oven at 325°F/160°C for 10 minutes.

STERILIZING IN BOILING WATER

19 FILLING & SEALING JARS

When using lidless jars, seal chutneys and pickles with vinegar-proof lids. For jams and other sweet preserves, use waxed paper disks and cellophane seals secured with a rubber band.

1 △ Use a ladle and jam funnel to fill the hot sterilized jar to within ½in (1cm) of the top. Wipe the rim clean with a damp cloth. Smooth a waxed paper disk onto the jam, waxed side down.

2 △ Wipe the cellophane disk with a wet cloth and place over the top of the jar, moist side up. Secure with a rubber band. When the disk is dry, it will shrink and create a tight seal.

20 SEALING BOTTLES WITH WAX

Glass bottles that contain liquid preserves must be sealed with a cork and hot wax to prevent contamination. Sterilize the bottle first before filling it. Use a stainless-steel ladle and a non-corrosive funnel to fill the bottle to within ½in (1cm) of the top.

Wax must cover neck of bottle as well as cork

Allow wax to set before applying more layers

1 △ Pour in hot liquid through a funnel. Soak the cork in hot water for a few minutes; push into bottle as far as it will go.

2 △ Tap in cork to within ¼in (5mm) of bottle top. When bottle is cold, tap cork level with top. Dip into melted wax.

3 △ After the first coat of wax is set, dip top of bottle several times into the melted wax to seal it completely.

21 PREPARING BOTTLES

If you want to heat-process a bottle, you must secure the cork with string. Fill the bottle using a funnel and wipe the rim clean. Soak the cork in hot water for a few minutes before pushing it in to within ¼in (5mm) of the top. Make a shallow cut in the cork.

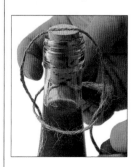

1 ◁ Cut a 20in (50cm) piece of string. Secure string in cut; loop around neck and insert string end through front of loop.

2 ▷ Pull both ends of the string down to tighten the loop. Tie the loose ends over the cork in a double knot.

22 CLAMP-TOP JAR

Both the clamp-top jar and its rubber seal must be sterilized before use to prevent contamination of the contents by molds or bacteria (*Tip 18*). If you want to keep the bottled preserve for longer than 3 months, the sealed jar must be heat-processed (*Tip 24*).

1 ◁ Place the new, sterilized rubber ring on the edge of the lid. Grip the lid tightly with one hand and fit the ring over it with the other.

2 ▷ Fill the hot, sterilized jar to within ½in (1cm) of the top or to the manufacturer's mark. Clamp the lid shut, using a cloth to hold it steady.

23 LID & SCREW-BAND JAR

The rubber-coated lid, screw band, and jar must all be sterilized before use (*Tip 18*). If you want to keep the bottled preserve for longer than 3 months, the sealed jar must be heat-processed (*Tip 24*). On cooling, the contents contract and a vacuum is formed.

1 ◁ Fill the hot, sterilized jar to within ½in (1cm) of the top. Wipe the rim, and cover with the sterilized, rubber-coated lid.

2 ▷ Hold the jar steady with a cloth. Screw the band down until it is tight, then release it by a quarter turn, or as directed by the manufacturer.

24 HEAT-PROCESSING

To heat-process a preserve, wrap each jar or bottle in a few layers of cloth or folded newspaper. Stand on a metal rack placed in a large, lidded pan. Pour in enough hot water to cover the lids or corks by at least 1in (2.5cm). Cover the pan and boil for the stated time (*see below*); check the water level occasionally. Remove from the water and tighten any screw bands. As the jar cools, a vacuum is formed.

Lid will dip in center if vacuum has formed

△ TO CHECK THE SEAL
Gently undo the clamp or screw band; grip the rim with your fingers. If it has sealed, it will support the weight.

HEAT-PROCESSING TIMES

Container	Cold-packed preserves	Hot-packed preserves
1lb (500g) jars	25 minutes	20 minutes
1 pint (500ml) bottles	25 minutes	20 minutes
2lb (1kg) jars	30 minutes	25 minutes
1¾–2 pint (1 liter) bottles	30 minutes	25 minutes

25 PREVENT DISCOLORATION

Some fruit discolor during drying (*Tip 26, Drying fruit*). Before drying, you can coat the fruit with an acidulated dip or a honey dip to prevent discoloration.

■ For an acidulated dip, add 6 tbsp lemon juice or 2 tbsp ascorbic acid crystals or powder to 4 cups (1 liter) warm water and mix together thoroughly.

■ For a honey dip, blend 1 cup (250g) each of honey and sugar with 1 cup (250ml) water in a heavy-based saucepan. Stir over a low heat to dissolve the sugar, then bring to a boil. Boil for a second or two, then remove from the heat; leave until cold.

26 Drying fruit

Dried fruit have a prolonged shelf life and simply need steeping in hot water to rehydrate. In hot weather, dry produce outside in full sun on muslin-covered trays over a period of 2–3 days, or hang up to dry in an airy room. To dry fruit in the oven, heat the oven to 225°F/110°C.

OVEN-DRYING FRUIT

Fruit	Preparation	Dip	Drying time
Apples	Peeled, if desired; cut into rings	Acidulated water	6–8 hours, until no moisture left
Apricots	Halved & pitted	Acidulated water	36–48 hours, until dry & leathery
Bananas	Peeled & halved lengthwise	Acidulated water	10–16 hours
Berries	Left whole	Dip in boiling water for a few seconds	12–18 hours
Cherries	Pitted, if desired	Dip in boiling water for a few seconds	18–24 hours
Citrus peel	Cut into long strips without pith	None	10–12 hours
Peaches	Peeled, pitted, halved, or sliced	Acidulated water	Halved: 36–48 hrs Sliced: 12–16 hrs
Pears	Peeled, if desired; halved & cored	Acidulated water	36–48 hours
Pineapple	Peeled, cored, sliced into rings	Honey	36–48 hours
Plums	Whole or halved; pitted	Dip in boiling water for a few seconds	Whole: 36–48 hrs Halved: 18–24 hrs
Strawberries	Halved	Honey	12–18 hours

27 Basic hygiene

All ingredients must be in prime condition without bruising or mold. Kitchen surfaces and utensils must be kept clean. Wipe surfaces with a sterilizing solution before you start, and as you work.

PRESERVING SKILLS

28 BLANCHING & SKINNING FRUIT

Blanching plays an important part in preserving fruit since it destroys enzymes that cause deterioration and discoloration on exposure to air. Blanch fruit briefly in boiling acidulated water, made by adding 3 tbsp vinegar or lemon juice, or 2 tsp citric acid, to every 4 cups (1 liter) water. After blanching, put the fruit into ice water to stop the cooking process.

SKINNING FRUIT
The easiest way to skin soft fruit is to blanch them in boiling water for a few seconds. Then peel off the skin with a knife.

PEELING LARGE CITRUS FRUIT
Slice off the two ends of the fruit. Working from top to bottom, cut away peel, pith, and skin, following the curve of the fruit.

29 PEELING CITRUS FRUIT

The peel and pith pull away easily from most citrus fruit, leaving the segments covered in fine skin. To remove peel, pith, and skin at the same time, use a serrated knife. For small citrus fruit, such as a lemon, cut around the fruit in a continuous spiral. For larger fruit, such as a grapefruit, see picture and caption at left. When preparing the rind for drying or candying, remove what pith and skin you can by hand.

30 WEIGHTING DOWN

Weighting down keeps the ingredients immersed in liquid, protecting them from deterioration through oxidation. Use non-porous objects that can be sterilized easily, such as a water-filled glass bottle or jar, or glazed plate. After weighting down, check that the liquid covers the ingredients by a minimum of ½in (1cm); add more if necessary.

WEIGHTING FRUIT
A plate fits snugly into the top of a bowl to keep soaking fruit immersed in liquid.

31 MAKING PECTIN STOCK

A jam or jelly requires pectin to set. If there is not enough pectin in the fruit, add pectin stock up to half the total volume of the fruit pulp. To make pectin stock, core 2lb (1kg) apples, setting aside the cores, and chop in a food processor. Place chopped fruit and cores in a preserving pan, cover with water, and bring to a boil. Simmer for 25–30 minutes or until soft. Strain through a jelly bag (*Tip 33*) and reserve the liquid. Return pulp to the pan, cover with water, and bring to a boil. Simmer for 30 minutes. Strain again. Combine both quantities of liquid in the pan. Boil rapidly for 10–15 minutes. Pour into sterilized bottles, then seal. Refrigerate; use within 1 week.

32 TESTING FOR PECTIN CONTENT

To test for pectin content in a jam or jelly, place 1 tbsp each of the cooked, unsweetened fruit juice and denatured alcohol (or 70% rubbing alcohol) in a bowl. Stir together for a few minutes until it starts to clot. Push your finger into the solution: a large clot indicates a high pectin content, while small clots indicate a low one.

FINGER TEST
After testing for pectin content, discard the mixture, because the alcohol is poisonous.

SUSPENDED JELLY BAG

33 USING A JELLY BAG

One of the principal skills in making jelly is to strain the fruit pulp through a sterilized jelly bag. Hang the bag from the upturned legs of a kitchen stool and place a large bowl underneath. Pour the fruit liquid and pulp into the bag and leave for 2–3 hours, or until it stops dripping. Some recipes may recommend leaving the pulp to drip overnight, but this is usually unnecessary. Do not squeeze the bag, or the jelly will be cloudy.

34 FILTERING

Even carefully prepared fruit liquids sometimes become cloudy and need filtering to remove small pieces of fruit, pith, or skin present in the liquid. To filter fruit liquids, use a sterilized jelly bag or a double layer of sterilized muslin, a thin layer of calico, or a coffee filter paper.

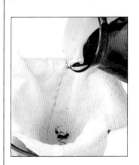

◁ **CLOTH FILTER**
Use a plastic sieve to hold in place the piece of muslin or calico when filtering the liquid.

▷ **PAPER FILTER**
When filtering a liquid into a jar through filter paper, support the filter in a plastic funnel.

35 MAKING A SPICE BAG

Enclosing whole spices or herbs in a retrievable muslin bag is a convenient way to add flavor to any preserve. Place the flavorings in the center of a small square of muslin, then draw up the corners to enclose the contents. Secure with kitchen string, and retrieve from the preserve after preparation.

FILLED SPICE BAG

Jams & Preserves

36 Making Jam

Jam-making is one of the simplest methods of preserving: you can use almost any fruit. A high concentration of sugar and acid in the mixture prevents bacteria and mold growth, while the reaction of sugar, acid, and pectin helps to create a good set. Most fruit have the right balance naturally, but you may sometimes need to correct the set (*Tip 39*) to achieve a satisfactory result.

PERFECTLY SET

37 What Can Go Wrong?

Many factors can affect the process of preserving and the end product.

- The jam has fermented: either too little sugar was added or equipment was not sterilized. Discard the jam.
- Fruit have risen to the top of the jam: the jam was not allowed to settle. Leave until cold, fold in the fruit evenly, and recan. Or, the syrup is too thin: drain it off, return to the pan with more sugar, reboil, and recan.
- The jam has crystallized: too much sugar was added. The jam will be very sweet but still edible.

Cooking Time
Cook the preserve for the exact time stated in the recipe. If cooked too long, the fruit will look dark as the sugar will caramelize; if too short, the preserve will ferment.

38 TESTING FOR SET

When a jam or similar preserve with a high sugar content is heated to 220°F/105°C, the sugar reacts with the pectin and setting begins. It is then ready to can. The setting point of the jam can be tested in three ways: by using a candy thermometer, or by the flake or wrinkle tests.

△ FLAKE TEST
Dip a metal spoon into the jam, then turn it so the jam runs off the side. The drops should run together and fall in flat sheets.

△ CANDY THERMOMETER
Warm the thermometer in a bowl of hot water before use so that the glass tube does not break. Clip it onto the side of the preserving pan, making sure the end is not touching the base of the pan. Boil the jam at a good rolling boil, until the thermometer registers 220°F/105°C.

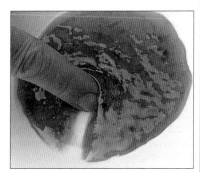

△ WRINKLE TEST
Pour a little hot jam onto a cold saucer and allow it to cool. Push the jam with a finger; if it wrinkles, it has reached setting point.

39 CORRECTING THE SET

If the jam or jelly will not set, it contains too little pectin. Test for pectin content (*Tip 32*) and add commercial pectin or pectin stock (*Tip 31*), then reboil until the setting point is reached. There is less pectin in frozen fruit than fresh. The jam might not set because of an incorrect balance between pectin and acid: add lemon juice and reboil.

40 EXOTIC FRUIT JAM
Makes about 3 pints (1.5kg)

Ingredients
1 medium pineapple, about
2½lb (1.25kg)
2lb (1kg) cooking apples
10oz (300g) fresh litchis or
14oz (425g) canned litchis
1 cup (250ml) water
Rind of 1 lemon
Juice of 2 lemons
5 cups (1.25kg) granulated
sugar
SHELF LIFE
2 years

1 △ Peel, core, and finely chop pineapple and apple. Peel, pit, and halve litchis. Transfer to a preserving pan and add drained litchis, water, lemon rind, and juice.

2 △ Bring mixture to a boil, then reduce heat and simmer for 20–25 minutes, or until apples have turned to a pulp and pineapple pieces have softened.

3 △ Add sugar to the pan and stir well over medium heat until it has dissolved completely. Increase heat and bring the mixture to a rapid, rolling boil.

4 ▷ Boil the fruit mixture rapidly for 20–25 minutes, stirring frequently until the jam starts to thicken as it reaches its setting point. Test for set (*Tip 38*). Skim off any froth as it rises to the surface of the jam.

5 △ Remove the preserving pan from the heat and leave for a few minutes to allow the jam to settle. Skim off any froth again if necessary. As the jam cools, it will begin to thicken and set.

6 ▷ Ladle the jam into hot, sterilized jars, then seal immediately with waxed paper disks and cellophane seals. The jam is ready to eat immediately, but improves with longer keeping.

ALTERNATIVE FRUIT
Other fruit – such as mango, papaya, or melon – can be used instead of pineapple, but use the same quantity of apple.

41 RASPBERRY JAM
Makes about 3 pints (1.5kg)

Ingredients
2 pints (1kg) raspberries
4 cups (1kg) granulated sugar
Juice of 1 lemon
SHELF LIFE
2 years

1 Layer the raspberries and sugar in a preserving pan. Cover with a cloth and leave overnight.
2 Next day, add the lemon juice. Bring slowly to a boil, stirring frequently until the sugar dissolves.
3 Increase the heat and boil rapidly for 20–25 minutes, until the setting point is reached (*Tip 38*). Stir constantly toward the end of cooking to prevent jam from sticking.
4 Remove the pan from the heat and allow the jam to settle for a few minutes. Ladle into hot jars, then seal.

42 BLUEBERRY JAM
Makes about 3 pints (1.5kg)

Ingredients
2 pints (1kg) blueberries
4 cups (1kg) granulated sugar
4 tbsp water
Juice of 1 lemon
SHELF LIFE
2 years

1 Put the blueberries, sugar, water, and lemon juice in a preserving pan. Bring slowly to a boil, stirring occasionally until the sugar has dissolved. Reduce the heat and simmer for about 10 minutes.
2 Increase the heat and boil rapidly for 15–20 minutes, until the setting point is reached (*Tip 38*).
3 Remove the pan from the heat and allow the jam to settle for a few minutes. Ladle into hot, sterilized jars, then seal.

Jam will set soft

43 PLUM JAM
Makes about 3½ pints (1.75kg)

Ingredients
2½ lb (1.25kg) plums
1½ cups (350ml) water
4 cups (1kg) granulated
sugar
SHELF LIFE
2 years

1 Halve and pit the plums; cut the plums into quarters if they are large. Put in a preserving pan with the water. Bring to a boil, reduce the heat, and simmer for about 25 minutes, stirring occasionally, until the plums are soft.
2 Add the sugar, stirring until it has dissolved. Return to a boil and boil for 25–30 minutes, until the setting point is reached (*Tip 38*).
3 Remove the pan from the heat and allow the jam to settle for a few minutes. Ladle the jam into hot, sterilized jars, then seal.

44 APRICOT JAM
Makes about 3 pints (1.5kg)

Ingredients
2½ lb (1.25kg) apricots
Juice of 1 lemon
4 cups (1kg) granulated
sugar
1¼ cups (300ml) water
SHELF LIFE
2 years

1 Halve the apricots; remove and reserve pits. Put apricots in a bowl and sprinkle with lemon juice. Mix well and cover.
2 Crack open 10 of the apricot pits with a hammer or nutcracker and extract kernels. Taste one – if it is very bitter, use only half of them. Blanch kernels for 1 minute in boiling water, then split into segments or chop finely.
3 Put sugar and water in preserving pan. Bring slowly to a boil, stirring until the sugar has dissolved, then boil rapidly for 3–4 minutes. Add apricots, return to a boil; simmer for 5 minutes.
4 Return to a boil and boil rapidly for 20–25 minutes, until the setting point is reached (*Tip 38*). Just before this point is reached and the jam is ready, stir in the prepared kernels.
5 Remove the pan from the heat and allow the jam to settle for a few minutes. Ladle the jam into hot, sterilized jars, then seal.

45 BLACKCURRANT JAM
Makes about 3 pints (1.5kg)

Ingredients
2 pints (1kg) blackcurrants
3 cups (750ml) water
3 cups (750g) granulated sugar
A little brandy, to seal
SHELF LIFE
2 years

1 Put blackcurrants and water in preserving pan. Bring slowly to a boil, then reduce heat and simmer for 20–25 minutes, stirring occasionally, until the mixture has reduced by one-third.
2 Add sugar to the pan. Slowly return to a boil, stirring until the sugar has dissolved, then boil rapidly for 15–20 minutes, until the setting point is reached (*Tip 38*). Remove the pan from the heat and allow to stand until the jam is cold.
3 Ladle the jam into hot, sterilized jars. Cover each jar with a waxed paper disk dipped in brandy, then seal.

46 DAMSON JAM
Makes about 3½ pints (1.75kg)

Ingredients
2½ lb (1.25kg) damsons
3 cups (750ml) water
Granulated sugar (Step 3)
SHELF LIFE
2 years

1 Put the whole, uncut damsons and water in a preserving pan and bring to a boil. Reduce the heat and simmer for about 25 minutes, stirring occasionally with a wooden spoon, until the fruit is mushy but not too liquid.
2 Let the mixture cool slightly, then sieve out the pits through a nylon sieve. Do not use a metal sieve since it might affect the color and flavor of the finished jam.
3 Measure the fruit pulp and add 2½ cups (625g) sugar for every 2 cups (500ml) pulp. Return the pulp with the sugar to the preserving pan and bring the mixture to a boil.
4 Boil for 10–15 minutes, until the setting point is reached (*Tip 38*).
5 Remove the pan from the heat and allow the jam to settle for a few minutes. Ladle the jam into hot, sterilized jars, then seal.

47 GRAPE JAM
Makes about 2½ pints (1.25kg)

Ingredients
2 lemons
2lb (1kg) seedless green
or red grapes
3 cups (750g) granulated
sugar
1 cup (100g) lightly
toasted pecans
⅓ cup (75ml) brandy

SHELF LIFE
2 years

1 Thinly slice the lemons and place with grapes and sugar in a preserving pan. Mix well, cover, and allow to stand for a few hours, until the juices start to run.

2 Bring the mixture to a boil, then cook over a moderate heat for 1–1½ hours, stirring frequently to prevent it from sticking to the bottom of the pan.

3 There is no need to test this jam for setting point: it is ready when it is thick enough for a wooden spoon drawn through the center of the mixture to leave a clear channel.

4 Remove the pan from the heat and allow the jam to settle for a few minutes. This stops the fruit from sinking, as it cools, to the bottom of the jar. Then stir in the pecans and brandy. Ladle the jam into hot, sterilized jars, then seal.

5 If you want this jam to have an orange flavor, thinly slice 3 oranges instead of the 2 lemons, and add dark rum or an orange-flavored liqueur in place of the brandy. For even more orange flavor, add 2–3 tablespoons of orange-flower water after the chosen alcohol.

> **CHANGING INGREDIENTS**
> *If you cannot get grapes, make this jam with figs, fresh dates, plums, peaches, or apricots. Prepare the jam in the same way, using either lemons or oranges to taste. Toasted walnuts or whole almonds can be used instead of pecans.*

48 BLACK CHERRY CONFITURE
Makes about 3 pints (1.5kg)

Ingredients
2½ lb (1.25kg) black
cherries
3 cups (750g) granulated
sugar
1 cup (250ml) blackcurrant
or redcurrant juice
4 tbsp kirsch or cherry
brandy
SHELF LIFE
2 years

THE BEST CHERRY
*Black cherry confiture is
best made with Morello
cherries, although any sour
black cherries can be used.*

1 Layer the cherries and sugar in the preserving pan. Add the blackcurrant or redcurrant juice; you can use the juice of 3 lemons instead of the currant juice if you prefer.
2 Cover the preserving pan, and allow to settle for a few hours.
3 Bring the mixture slowly to a boil, occasionally shaking the pan gently. Skim well, then boil for 20–25 minutes, or until the setting point is reached. Test for set (*Tip 38*).
4 Remove the pan from the heat and allow the fruit to settle for a few minutes.
5 Stir in the kirsch or brandy.
6 While the mixture is still hot, ladle the jam into hot, sterilized jars, then seal and store. Like any preserve, black cherry confiture can be eaten immediately, but improves with age if stored in a cool place.

49 WILD STRAWBERRY CONFITURE
Makes about 2½ pints (1.25kg)

Ingredients
2 pints (1kg) wild strawberries
3 cups (750g) granulated
sugar
1 cup (250ml) 80 proof
vodka
SHELF LIFE
6 months

1 Layer the wild strawberries and sugar in a large glass bowl, starting and finishing with a layer of sugar. Pour in the vodka, cover with a clean cloth, and allow to stand overnight.
2 Next day, drain liquid into a preserving pan. Bring to a boil; boil rapidly for a few minutes, or until the mixture reaches 240°F/116°C on a candy thermometer.
3 Add the strawberries. Return to a boil; boil for 5–7 minutes, or until setting point is reached.
4 Remove from heat and allow to settle for a few minutes. Skim well. Ladle into hot jars; seal.

50 ORANGE MARMALADE

Makes about 4 pints (2kg)

Ingredients

2lb (1kg) Seville oranges
2 lemons
8 cups (2 liters) water
6 cups (1.5kg) granulated sugar
⅓ cup (75ml) dry orange liqueur, such as Triple Sec (optional)

SHELF LIFE

2 years

1 Scrub the citrus fruit well to remove any wax coating. Cut in half.
2 Remove and reserve seeds. Slice fruit crosswise into thin semi-circles; tie seeds in a muslin bag; put fruit and muslin bag in a large glass bowl with the water. Cover and leave overnight.
3 Next day, transfer the fruit and water to a preserving pan. Bring to a boil, then reduce heat and simmer for 45 minutes to 1 hour, or until the orange rind is just soft and the mixture has reduced by half.
4 Add sugar to the pan. Slowly return to a boil, stirring until the sugar has dissolved. Skim well.
5 Boil the mixture rapidly for 10–15 minutes, or until the setting point is reached.
6 Remove the pan from heat. Allow fruit to settle for a few minutes.
7 Add the liqueur, if using; stir to distribute evenly through mixture. Ladle marmalade into hot, sterilized jars, then seal.

SPICE IT UP
Try adding some coriander to orange marmalade (left) to give it an additional spicy orange flavor. Stir in 3 tbsp crushed seeds at the end of Step 4 above, before boiling the mixture to setting point.

51 PEACH MARMALADE WITH VANILLA

Makes about 2 pints (1kg)

Ingredients
2½ lb (1.25kg) white or
yellow peaches
4 cups (1kg) granulated
sugar
Juice of 2 lemons
4 tbsp good-quality cognac
1–2 vanilla pods

SHELF LIFE
1 year

1 Skin the peaches by blanching them in boiling water (*Tip 28*). Halve them, remove the pits, and cut the flesh into thick slices.

2 Place the peach slices in a preserving pan with the sugar and lemon juice. Cover and allow to stand for a few hours.

3 Bring mixture to a boil, then reduce the heat and simmer gently for 20 minutes, until the peaches are just soft.

4 Return to a boil and boil rapidly, stirring frequently, for 20–25 minutes, until the setting point is reached (*Tip 38*). The peaches produce a soft-set marmalade.

5 Remove the pan from the heat, skim the mixture well, and allow it to cool for about 10 minutes. Then stir in the cognac.

6 Cut the vanilla pods into 2–3in (5–7cm) lengths.

7 Ladle the preserve into hot, sterilized jars, inserting pieces of vanilla pod into each; seal.

8 The marmalade will be ready to eat in approximately 1 month, but improves with longer keeping.

SKIM WELL
Make sure that you skim the vanilla-flavored peach marmalade thoroughly at every stage of the cooking process, since peaches tend to produce a large amount of froth.

52 RICH MINCEMEAT

Makes about 5 pints (2.5kg)

Ingredients

2 medium cooking apples
½lb (200g) carrots
¾ cup (125g) each of fresh ginger root, dried apricots, glacé cherries, & prunes
Zest & juice of 2 lemons & 2 oranges
1½ cups (250g) each of raisins, golden raisins, & currants
1¼ cups (175g) mixed candied peel
½ cup (125g) honey or dark brown sugar
2–3 tbsp pumpkin pie spice
1 cup (250ml) brandy

SHELF LIFE
2 years

SUPERIOR PEEL
If possible, choose whole candied citrus peel rather than prechopped peel, and dice it yourself. Alternatively, make your own candied citrus peel (Tip 78).

1 Coarsely grate apples; finely grate carrots and fresh ginger root; coarsely chop apricots, cherries, and prunes.

2 Put all the ingredients in a large bowl and mix very well. Cover with a clean cloth and allow to stand in a warm kitchen for 2–3 days.

3 Pack the mincemeat tightly into sterilized jars and cover with waxed paper disks. Pour 1–2 tablespoons of brandy into each jar, then seal.

4 Every 6 months or so, open the jars, pour in a little brandy over the top, and reseal.

JELLIES

53 RASPBERRY JELLY
Makes about 4 pints (2kg)

Ingredients
1lb (500g) cooking apples
2 pints (1kg) raspberries
2 cups (500ml) water
Granulated sugar (Step 3)
Juice of 1 lemon
Scented geranium leaves
(optional)
A little brandy
SHELF LIFE
2 years

1 △ Remove cores from apples and set aside. Coarsely chop apples. Wash raspberries and place with apples in food processor. Process in batches until all fruit are finely chopped.

2 △ Put fruit and cores in a preserving pan. Cover with water. Bring to a boil, then simmer for 20–30 minutes until soft and pulpy. Pour fruit and liquid into a sterilized jelly bag (*Tip 33*).

3 △ Leave jelly bag for 2–3 hours, or until it stops dripping. Measure juice and allow 2 cups (500g) sugar for every 2 cups (500ml) juice. Return juice to cleaned pan; add sugar and lemon juice.

4 △ Heat gently, stirring occasionally, until sugar has dissolved. Bring liquid to a rapid boil. Skim well with slotted spoon to remove froth. Boil rapidly to setting point (*Tip 38*).

54 SUCCESSFUL JELLIES

Three elements transform dull, cloudy fruit juice into clear, sparkling jelly: pectin, acidity, and sugar.
- Supplement low-pectin fruit, such as strawberries, with pectin-rich ones, such as apples or currants.
- Some recipes suggest allowing the pulp to drip through the jelly bag overnight, but this is usually unnecessary. Leave it until it stops dripping, usually after a few hours.
- To extract more liquid from the fruit after it has dripped once, return pulp to the preserving pan, add water to cover, simmer gently for 30 minutes, then let it drip again. Add juice to the first batch.

5 △ Ladle jelly through a jam funnel into hot, sterilized jars. Allow to cool until semi-set, then, if using, insert a geranium leaf into center of each jar. Cover each jar with a waxed paper disk dipped in a little brandy, then seal.

CLEAR JELLY
Before sealing, prick any air bubbles that appear in the jelly with a wooden skewer.

55 MINTED APPLE JELLY
Makes about 2½ pints (1.25kg)

Ingredients
Small bunch of mint
Few strips of lemon peel
2lb (1kg) apples
7 cups (1.75 liters) water
or dry cider
Granulated sugar (Step 4)
Juice of 1 lemon
3–4 tbsp finely chopped
fresh mint
A little brandy
SHELF LIFE
2 years

1 Tie the mint and lemon peel together with string. Put in a preserving pan with the apples and 5 cups (1.25 liters) of water or cider.
2 Bring to a boil; simmer, stirring occasionally, for about 25 minutes, or until apples are pulpy. Pour into a sterilized jelly bag (*Tip 33*); leave for 2–3 hours, or until it stops dripping.
3 Remove the pulp from the jelly bag and return it to the cleaned pan. Add the remaining water or cider. Bring to a boil, then simmer for 20 minutes. Drip through the jelly bag.
4 Combine the two batches of juice and measure it. Allow 2 cups (500g) sugar for every 2 cups (500ml) juice. Pour the juice into the cleaned preserving pan and add lemon juice.
5 Bring to a boil; boil for about 10 minutes. Add the sugar, stirring until it has dissolved, and boil rapidly for 8–10 minutes, until the setting point is reached (*Tip 38*).
6 Remove the pan from the heat, and allow to cool for about 10 minutes. Stir in the chopped mint, then pour into hot, sterilized jars and allow to cool completely. Cover each jar with a waxed paper disk dipped in a little brandy, then seal.

KEEP THE CORES
There is no need to core the apples if you chop them by hand. If you use a processor, remove the cores first but later add them to the pan, since they contain pectin.

56 HOT CRABAPPLE JELLY
Makes about 2½ pints (1.25kg)

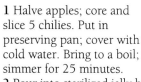

Ingredients
2lb (1kg) crabapples
10 fresh red chilies
Granulated sugar (Step 2)
A little brandy
SHELF LIFE
2 years

1 Halve apples; core and slice 5 chilies. Put in preserving pan; cover with cold water. Bring to a boil; simmer for 25 minutes.
2 Pour into sterilized jelly bag (*Tip 33*); drip for 2–3 hours. Measure juice: allow 2 cups (500g) sugar for every 2 cups (500ml).
3 Put juice and sugar in pan; bring slowly to boil, stirring until sugar has dissolved. Reduce heat and skim. Return to boil for 15 minutes, until setting point is reached (*Tip 38*). Remove pan from heat, allow to settle. Skim well. Pour liquid into hot, sterilized jars; insert 1 chili into each when semi-set. Cover with a waxed disk dipped in brandy; seal.

57 REDCURRANT JELLY
Makes about 4 pints (2kg)

Ingredients
2 pints (1kg) redcurrants
2 cups (600ml) water
Granulated sugar (Step 2)
Juice of 1 lemon
A little brandy
SHELF LIFE
2 years

SEAL WITH BRANDY
Dip each waxed paper seal briefly in a little brandy to preserve the jelly perfectly.

1 Put fruit and water in a preserving pan and bring to a boil. Reduce the heat and simmer for 20–30 minutes, crushing the fruit against the pan, until pulpy.
2 Pour fruit and liquid into a sterilized jelly bag (*Tip 33*). Leave for 2–3 hours, or until it stops dripping. Measure juice: allow 2 cups (500g) sugar for every 2 cups (500ml).
3 Put juice, sugar, lemon juice in pan. Heat gently, stirring until sugar has dissolved. Bring to a boil, reduce the heat, and skim well. Return to a rapid boil for 10 minutes, until setting point is reached (*Tip 38*). Pour liquid into hot, sterilized jars; seal.

58 RED PLUM JELLY
Makes about 2½ pints (1.25kg)

Ingredients
2lb (1kg) red plums
15 bitter almonds or
1 tsp bitter almond extract
Granulated sugar (Step 4)
4 tbsp slivovitz or other
plum brandy
Blanched bitter almonds
(optional)
SHELF LIFE
2 years

1 Put plums in preserving pan. Add coarsely pounded almonds or extract to pan; cover with cold water.
2 Bring to a boil; reduce heat and simmer for 20–25 minutes until pulpy.
3 Pour fruit and liquid into jelly bag; allow to drip for 2–3 hours (*Tip 33*).
4 Measure juice: allow 2 cups (500g) sugar for every 2 cups (500ml). Put juice and sugar in pan, bring to boil, stirring until sugar has dissolved. Boil for a few minutes, then reduce heat, skim. Boil for 10 minutes until setting point is reached.
5 Allow to cool. Skim well, stir in slivovitz, pour into jars. Add a few almonds to each jar, then seal.

59 PINEAPPLE & ORANGE JELLY
Makes about 2½ pints (1.25kg)

Ingredients
1 small pineapple, about
1lb (500g)
1lb (500g) apples
2 oranges
6 cups (1.5 liters) water
Granulated sugar (Step 3)
SHELF LIFE
2 years

1 Slice fruit. Add to preserving pan with water. Bring to a boil; reduce heat, simmer for 30 minutes until pulpy.
2 Pour fruit and liquid into jelly bag and leave for 2–3 hours, or until it stops dripping (*Tip 33*).
3 Remove pulp from bag, return to pan, cover with cold water. Boil, simmer, and drip as above. Combine both batches and measure: allow 2 cups (500g) sugar for every 2 cups (500ml) juice.
4 Put juice and sugar in cleaned pan. Bring to a boil, stirring to dissolve sugar. Boil for a few minutes, reduce heat, skim well. Return to a boil for 10–12 minutes until setting point is reached. Allow to settle; skim, bottle, and seal.

FRUIT IN SYRUP OR ALCOHOL

60 RASPBERRY SYRUP

Makes about 3 cups (750ml)

Ingredients

2 pints (1kg) raspberries
⅓ cup (75ml) water
Granulated sugar (Step 3)

SHELF LIFE
2 years

RIPE FRUIT
Making syrup is a good way of using up soft fruit that are too ripe for jams or jellies. Any ripe, juicy berries can be used, but discard any berries that are bruised or moldy.

1 Put raspberries and water in a heatproof bowl and mash well. Set over a pan of simmering water, mashing occasionally, for 1 hour.
2 Pour into a sterilized jelly bag and leave for a few hours, or until it stops dripping (*Tip 33*). Squeeze the bag to extract as much fruit liquid as possible. Filter the juice through a double layer of sterilized muslin into a measuring cup (*Tip 34*).
3 Measure the juice and allow 1½ cups (400g) sugar for every 2 cups (500ml). Put in a pan and bring slowly to a boil, stirring occasionally until the sugar has dissolved.
4 Skim off the froth and boil for 4–5 minutes. Do not overcook, or the mixture will start to set.
5 Pour into hot, sterilized bottles, and cork. Allow to cool, then seal with wax (*Tip 20*).
6 Serve raspberry syrup over desserts or ice cream, or dilute with water to make a cold drink.

61 POMEGRANATE SYRUP
Makes about 2 cups (500ml)

Ingredients
*4lb (2kg) red
pomegranates
1½ cups (400g) granulated
sugar
1 tsp orange-flower water
(optional)*
SHELF LIFE
2 years

1 Cut pomegranates in half horizontally; use a lemon squeezer to extract juice.
2 Filter juice through a double layer of muslin (*Tip 34*) into a pan. Add sugar and bring slowly to a boil, stirring until it has dissolved.
3 Boil for 10 minutes; remove from heat, skim well, and stir in orange-flower water, if using. Pour syrup into a hot, sterilized bottle, then seal.

62 PINEAPPLE IN KIRSCH
Makes about 2lb (1kg)

Ingredients
*4–5 baby pineapples
3–4 cinnamon sticks
3–4 strips orange peel
2 cups (500g) granulated
sugar
5–6 blanched bitter
almonds (optional)
About 4 cups (1 liter)
kirsch*
SHELF LIFE
2 years

1 Peel, core, and cut the baby pineapples into rings ½in (1cm) thick.
2 Arrange pineapple rings with cinnamon sticks and orange peel in a sterilized jar – a decorative jar is nice, if you have one.
3 Add sugar and blanched bitter almonds, if using. If you would like the pineapple to be sweeter, increase amount of sugar to a maximum of 2 cups (500g), according to taste.
4 Pour enough kirsch into the jar to cover all the fruit and flavorings, then seal.
5 Store in a cool, dark place for 2–3 months. For the first few weeks, shake the jar every few days to help dissolve the sugar.
6 Serve as a dessert, with its syrup and cream or ice cream.

DIFFERENT SPIRITS
The cherry flavor of kirsch enhances the pineapple, but you can use vodka, eau de vie, or white rum instead.

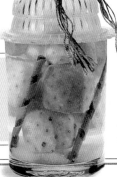

63 CLEMENTINES IN BRANDY
Makes about 4lb (2kg)

Ingredients
4lb (2kg) clementines
4 cups (1kg) granulated sugar
8 cups (2 liters) water
2½in (6cm) piece fresh ginger root
2 tsp whole cloves
Clementine leaves, washed & dried (optional)
About 2 cups (500ml) brandy

SHELF LIFE
2 years

1 Wash the clementines well in hot, soapy water to remove any wax coating, then dry thoroughly. Prick fruit in a few places with a wooden skewer.

2 Put sugar and water in a preserving pan.

3 Make a spice bag (*Tip 35*) with 2in (5cm) shredded ginger root, 1 tsp cloves, and 1 clementine leaf, if using; add to pan. Bring to a boil and boil rapidly for 5 minutes. Add clementines, return to a boil, then simmer very gently for about 1 hour or until soft when pierced with a knife.

4 Lift the fruit out of the syrup with a slotted spoon. Arrange in hot, sterilized jars, adding a few shreds of ginger root, a few cloves, and clementine leaves, if using, to each jar.

5 Bring the syrup to a boil and boil rapidly until it reaches 235°F/113°C on a candy thermometer. Allow to cool to 167°F/75°C.

6 Pour in enough brandy to half-fill the jars. Top up with the syrup, then seal. The clementines will be ready to eat in 1 month, but improve with keeping.

KUMQUATS IN BRANDY
Instead of clementines, use the same quantity of kumquats. Wash and prick the fruit and cook for about 25 minutes, or until soft, then continue as for the main recipe.

64 PEACHES IN BRANDY

Makes about 2lb (1kg)

Ingredients

3lb (1.5kg) firm peaches
4 cups (1 liter) water
6 cups (1.5kg) granulated
sugar
1 vanilla pod, small piece
cinnamon stick, 4 cloves,
& 3–4 cardamom pods,
made into a spice bag
1⅓ cups (300ml) brandy
½ cup (100g) glacé cherries
(optional)

SHELF LIFE
2 years

1 △ Blanch, skin, halve peaches (*Tip 28*). Put water and one-third sugar into pan; boil; simmer for 5 minutes to make syrup.

2 △ Slide peach halves into syrup, return to boil, then simmer for 4–5 minutes. Remove peaches and let cool.

3 △ Put 2½ cups (600ml) syrup in a pan with rest of sugar and spice bag. Boil until it reaches 219°F/104°C. Cool, remove spice bag, stir in brandy. Set a cherry in each peach half, if using; put in hot, sterilized jar. Pour in syrup; seal.

65 PEARS IN EAU DE VIE
Makes about 2lb (1kg)

Ingredients
3–4 ripe pears
1¼–1½ cups (325–375g)
granulated sugar
1 vanilla pod
4 cups (1 liter) eau de vie
SHELF LIFE
2 years

1 Wash the pears, dry, and prick in a few places with a wooden skewer.
2 Arrange pears in a sterilized jar. Add sugar and vanilla pod; pour in enough eau de vie to cover the pears. Seal.
3 Store in a cool, dark place for 3–4 months. For the first few weeks, shake jar every few days to help dissolve the sugar.

66 CASSIS (BLACKCURRANT LIQUEUR)
Makes about 4 cups (1 liter)

Ingredients
2lb (1kg) blackcurrants
2 cups (500ml) brandy
1½–2 cups (350–500g)
granulated sugar
SHELF LIFE
Indefinite; once opened, consume within 3 months

AGE IMPROVES IT
Cassis can be enjoyed as soon as it is bottled, but it improves with keeping. Other berries can be used to make this liqueur instead of blackcurrants.

1 Wash blackcurrants, place them in a sterilized jar, and crush well.
2 Pour in brandy, then cover jar tightly. Leave in a cool, dark place for about 2 months, shaking jar occasionally.
3 Pour fruit and liquid into a sterilized jelly bag; leave for a few hours, until it stops dripping (*Tip 33*). Squeeze bag to extract as much liquid as possible. Filter juice through a double layer of muslin (*Tip 34*), then return to jar.
4 Add sugar according to taste, then seal. Leave in a cool, dark place for 2 weeks, shaking jar every few days until all the sugar has dissolved and the liquid is clear.
5 Filter the liquid again if necessary. Pour into sterilized bottles, then seal.

BUTTERS, CURDS, & CHEESES

67 MANGO BUTTER
Makes 3 pints (1.5kg)

Ingredients
4lb (2kg) ripe mangoes
1⅓ cups (300ml) sweet cider or water
Zest & juice of 2 lemons
4 cups (1kg) granulated sugar
SHELF LIFE
2 years

FRUIT BUTTER LAYERS
Mango butter can be layered with Orchard and Kiwi fruit butters in a jar (Tip 70).

1 Cut mango flesh into large chunks; place with cider or water in a preserving pan. Bring to a boil, then simmer for 15–20 minutes, until the fruit is pulpy. Press mixture through a sieve or pass it through a food mill. Return purée to pan.
2 Add lemon zest, lemon juice, and sugar to pan, stirring until sugar has dissolved. Bring to a boil; simmer for 35–40 minutes, stirring often, until thickened. Pour into hot, sterilized jars; seal.

68 ORCHARD FRUIT BUTTER

Makes about 3 pints (1.5kg)

Ingredients
2½lb (1.25kg) apples
1¼lb (625g) pears
1¼lb (625g) peaches
4 cups (1 liter) sweet cider
or water
4 cups (1kg) light brown or
white sugar
1 tsp whole allspice
½ tsp whole cloves
2 tsp ground cinnamon
SHELF LIFE
2 years

1 Chop apples and pears (no need to peel or core); halve and pit peaches. Put in a preserving pan with cider or water. Bring to a boil, skim, reduce the heat, and simmer for 1 hour, until the fruit is very soft and mushy.
2 Press the fruit through a sieve or pass it through a food mill. Return the purée to the cleaned pan. Add the sugar, stirring until it has dissolved. Bring to a boil, then simmer, stirring frequently, for 1½–2 hours, until the mixture has reduced and become very thick.
3 Grind the allspice and cloves in a spice mill or coffee grinder. Add to the pan with the cinnamon; continue to cook for a minute or two. Pour into hot, sterilized jars; seal.

69 KIWI FRUIT BUTTER

Makes about 2 pints (1kg)

Ingredients
2lb (1kg) ripe kiwi fruit
3 cups (750ml) dry cider
or water
Juice & zest of 1 lemon
5 tbsp (75g) fresh,
shredded ginger root
Granulated sugar (Step 2)
1 tsp freshly ground black
pepper (optional)
SHELF LIFE
2 years

1 Chop the unpeeled kiwi fruit and put in a preserving pan with cider or water and lemon juice. Bring to a boil, skim, reduce the heat, and simmer for 15–20 minutes, until the fruit is soft and mushy.
2 Press the mixture through a sieve or pass it through a food mill. Measure the purée: allow 1½ cups (400g) sugar for every 2 cups (500ml). Return purée to the cleaned pan.
3 Add shredded ginger root to pan with lemon zest, sugar, and pepper, if using, stirring until the sugar has dissolved. Bring to a boil, then simmer, stirring frequently, for 30–35 minutes, until the butter has reached the consistency of soft-set jam. Pour into hot, sterilized jars; seal.

70 FRUIT BUTTER LAYERS

To make a decorative layered preserve, place about 1¼ cups (300g) Kiwi fruit butter (*Tip 69*) in a small pan and heat gently until it comes to a boil. To prevent burning, add 1–2 tablespoons water. Pour it into a large, hot, sterilized jar and allow it to cool. Repeat with the Orchard fruit butter (*Tip 68*) and Mango butter (*Tip 67*), gradually filling up the jar with each layer. When the jar is full, cover the surface of the Mango butter with a waxed paper disk dipped in a little brandy, and then seal. This preserve has a shelf life of up to 2 years.

Cover the sealed jar with a circle of colored paper or fabric tied with string _____

Mango butter can be flavored with orange, vanilla, or cinnamon _____

Orchard fruit butter is lightly spiced with a warming hint of allspice, cloves, and cinnamon _____

Kiwi fruit butter has a slightly sharp taste _____

VARY THE INGREDIENTS
Try using different combinations of fruit when making Orchard fruit butter, but at least half the quantity of fruit must be apples. Any type will do, from dessert to windfalls.

71 PINK GRAPEFRUIT CURD

Makes about 2 pints (1kg)

Ingredients
*2 ruby red or pink
grapefruits
Juice of 2 lemons
1½ cups (400g) granulated
sugar
7 tbsp (100g) butter
4 eggs & 2 egg yolks
3 tbsp orange-flower water*

SHELF LIFE
3 months, refrigerated;
6 months,
heat-processed

1 Grate rind of 1 grapefruit; squeeze the juice. Peel and segment other grapefruit. Put zest, juice, and flesh, lemon juice, and sugar in a small pan. Heat gently, stirring until the sugar has dissolved. Add the butter; stir until melted.
2 Put in bowl placed over pan of simmering water. Beat eggs and yolks; sieve into mixture. Cook gently, stirring often, 25–40 minutes, until mixture coats back of spoon. Remove from heat; stir in orange water. Pour into hot, sterilized jars; seal.

72 SUCCESSFUL FRUIT CURD

The secret of making a good fruit curd is patience, since you must wait for it to thicken. Heat the curd gently over a pan of barely simmering water, and stir often so that the heat is evenly distributed. Do not hurry the process, or it will curdle and cannot be rescued.

73 LEMON CURD

Makes about 1½ pints (750g)

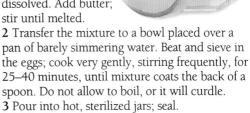

Ingredients
Zest & juice of 6 lemons
1½ cups (400g) granulated sugar
¾ cup (150g) butter
5 eggs

SHELF LIFE
3 months, refrigerated

1 Put zest and juice in small pan with sugar; heat gently, stirring until sugar has dissolved. Add butter; stir until melted.

2 Transfer the mixture to a bowl placed over a pan of barely simmering water. Beat and sieve in the eggs; cook very gently, stirring frequently, for 25–40 minutes, until mixture coats the back of a spoon. Do not allow to boil, or it will curdle.

3 Pour into hot, sterilized jars; seal.

---

74 QUINCE CHEESE

Makes about 4½ lb (2.25kg)

Ingredients
3lb (1.5kg) ripe quinces
8 cups (2 liters) water or dry cider
2–3 strips lemon peel
Juice of ½ lemon
Granulated sugar (Step 1)
Almond or peanut oil
Superfine sugar

SHELF LIFE
2 years

STORING FRUIT CHEESES
Arrange cheeses in layers between sheets of waxed paper in an airtight tin.

1 Wash quinces, then chop coarsely. Put in a preserving pan with enough water or dry cider to cover. Add lemon peel and juice. Bring to a boil, then simmer for 30–45 minutes, until fruit is soft and mushy. Press mixture through a sieve. Measure purée: allow 1½ cups (400g) sugar for every 2 cups (500ml).

2 Return fruit purée to cleaned pan; add sugar. Bring slowly to a boil, stirring until sugar has dissolved. Reduce heat; simmer mixture, stirring frequently, for 2½–3 hours until it is very thick. Remove from heat; allow to cool slightly.

3 Brush a baking tray with oil. Pour cheese into tray; smooth to an even layer. Allow to cool, then cover with a cloth. Leave for 24 hours.

4 Loosen cheese with palette knife, then turn out onto waxed paper. Cut into shapes and dust with superfine sugar. Allow to dry.

75 PEAR & TOMATO CHEESE
Makes about 2½ lb (1.25kg)

Ingredients
1½ lb (750g) ripe pears
½ lb (250g) apples
1kg (2lb) plum tomatoes
1 lemon
2 cups (500ml) water
Granulated sugar (Step 2)
1 tsp freshly ground black
pepper
1 tsp ground coriander
½ tsp ground cinnamon
¼ tsp ground cloves
SHELF LIFE
2 years in sealed jars

1 Core pears and apples; coarsely chop all fruit and place with water in a preserving pan. Bring to a boil, then reduce heat and simmer for about 30 minutes, until fruit is soft and mushy.
2 Press mixture through a sieve or pass through a food mill. Measure purée: allow 1½ cups (400g) sugar for every 2 cups (500ml).
3 Return purée to the cleaned pan; add sugar and spices. Bring to a boil, then simmer, stirring frequently, for 1–1½ hours, until the mixture has reduced and become very thick.
4 Pour into hot, sterilized jars, then seal.

76 FRUIT LEATHERS
Makes about 5oz (150g)

Ingredients
2lb (1kg) fully ripe fruit,
such as mangoes, litchis,
apricots, or peaches
1 tbsp lemon juice
2–3 tbsp sugar
SHELF LIFE
2 years

1 Peel and pit fruit, where necessary. Purée flesh in a food processor or food mill. Add lemon juice and sugar, stirring until sugar has dissolved.
2 Line a large, dampened baking tray with plastic wrap or foil, allowing about 1in (2.5cm) to hang over. Pour purée onto tray and spread in an even layer about ¼in (5mm) thick.
3 Preheat oven to 225°F/110°C. Place tray in oven and leave for about 12–14 hours with the oven door slightly ajar, until the purée is dry but still pliable.
4 Allow the leather to cool, then peel off plastic or foil. Roll leather up in waxed paper. Store in an airtight container.

DRIED & CANDIED FRUIT

77 OVEN-DRIED PEACHES

Makes 12 halves

Ingredients

6 yellow- or white-flesh peaches

SHELF LIFE
2 months

1 △ Blanch peaches in boiling water for a few seconds (*Tip 28*). Refresh in cold water, then peel off the skin. Halve the peaches and remove the pits. If large, cut again into quarters.

2 △ As the peaches are prepared, place them in a bowl of acidulated water to prevent discoloration during drying (*Tip 25*). When you are ready to dry the fruit, lift out and drain well.

78 CANDIED CITRUS PEEL

Makes about 3lb (1.5kg)

Ingredients

2lb (1kg) citrus peel
1½ cups (350ml) water
4 cups (1kg) granulated sugar

SHELF LIFE

1 year, crystallized; 2 years in syrup

1 Cut peel into 2in (5cm) strips. Put in pan; cover with water. Bring to a boil; simmer for 10 minutes. Drain, discard cooking liquid, and cover with fresh water. Return to a boil; reduce the heat and simmer for 20 minutes. Drain again.

2 Put peel in a large bowl and cover with cold water; leave for 24 hours.

3 Drain peel. Put water and sugar in a pan. Bring to a boil, stirring until sugar has dissolved. Add peel, reduce heat, and simmer gently for 2–3 hours until peel is translucent and most of the syrup is absorbed.

4 To preserve in syrup, spoon into sterilized jar, then seal.

5 For crystallized peel, lift out of syrup, arrange on wire racks, and dry in oven at 250°F/ 120°C for 12–24 hours, leaving door ajar. When cool, dust with superfine sugar.

3 △ Preheat oven to 225°F/110°C. Arrange pieces cut-side down on wire rack set over foil-lined baking tray. Place tray in oven, leaving door slightly ajar. Leave halves for 24–36 hrs, quarters for 12–16 hrs, smaller pieces for 8–12 hrs.

4 △ Turn the pieces over when they are halfway through drying. When dry, allow to cool and arrange in layers, between pieces of waxed paper, in an airtight container. Store in a cool place.

79 CANDIED PINEAPPLE RINGS

Makes about 2lb (1kg)

Ingredients
1 large pineapple
4 cups (1kg) granulated sugar
Juice of 1 lemon
Superfine sugar
SHELF LIFE
1 year

1 ▷ Peel, slice pineapple. Put in pan; cover with water. Bring to a boil; reduce heat; simmer for 15–20 minutes. Drain well; put in glass bowl. Strain 4 cups (1 liter) of cooking liquid into same pan. Add 1 cup (250g) sugar and lemon juice. Bring to a boil; boil rapidly for 2–3 minutes. Ladle hot syrup over rings; weight down (*Tip 30*); let stand 24 hours.

2 △ Day 2: drain rings; return syrup to pan. Add ½ cup (100g) sugar; bring to boil. Boil for 1–2 minutes; skim; ladle over rings; weight down; leave 24 hours. Day 3: repeat.

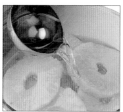

3 △ Day 4: as Day 2, add ¾ cup (150g) sugar. Day 5: repeat Day 4. Day 6: as Day 2, using remaining sugar. Leave for 48 hours. Day 8: simmer fruit and syrup in pan for 5 minutes.

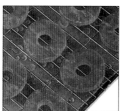

4 △ Arrange rings on rack over baking tray. Place in oven at 250°F/ 120°C, leaving door ajar, for 12–24 hours until fruit are dry. Allow to cool; dust with superfine sugar.

80 CANDIED APRICOTS

Makes about 3lb (1.5kg)

Ingredients

6 cups (1.5kg) sugar
1 cup (250ml) water
Juice of 1 lemon or
1 tsp citric acid
2lb (1kg) apricots

SHELF LIFE
3–4 months, crystallized;
2 years in syrup

CRYSTALLIZED APRICOTS
Drain the fruit from the syrup and dry on a rack for 24 hours. Dust with superfine sugar, then dry in oven for 12–24 hours at 250°F/120°C.

---

1 Put 4 cups (1kg) sugar in a preserving pan with water and lemon juice or citric acid. Bring to a boil, stirring until sugar has dissolved. Skim well; boil until it reaches 230°F/110°C on candy thermometer.
2 Prick each apricot. Slide into pan; simmer for 3 minutes. Remove with slotted spoon and place in a large glass bowl. Return syrup to a boil; boil for 5 minutes. Pour over apricots, weight down (*Tip 30*), and leave for 24 hours.
3 Drain apricots. Return syrup to pan, adding 1 cup (250g) sugar. Bring slowly to a boil; stir often. Skim well; boil for about 5 minutes.
4 Add apricots to pan. Return to a boil, reduce heat, and simmer gently for 5 minutes. Remove apricots and place in bowl. Bring syrup back to a boil; boil for 5 minutes. Pour over apricots, weight down, and leave for 24 hours.
5 Drain apricots. Return syrup to pan and add remaining sugar. Bring to a boil. Skim; boil for 2–3 minutes. Add apricots to pan. Return to a boil; reduce heat to a minimum; simmer gently for 3–4 hours until fruit is clear. Place fruit in sterilized jar; add syrup; seal.

81 ABOUT CANDYING

The process of candying replaces a fruit's moisture with a saturated sugar solution. Fruit are candied by steeping them in an increasingly concentrated syrup, a process that must be carried out slowly, otherwise the fruit will shrink and toughen. The candied fruit can then be crystallized by drying them in a low oven for many hours and then dusted with superfine sugar.

△ **SWEET FINALE**
Candied or crystallized fruit make ideal desserts.

VINEGARS

82 CITRUS VINEGAR
Makes about 4 cups (1 liter)

Ingredients
*4 cups (1 liter) white wine
(or cider) vinegar
3–4 oranges or lemons*
SHELF LIFE
2 years

1 Put vinegar in a non-corrosive pan. Boil rapidly for 1–2 minutes. Remove from heat; cool to 104°F/40°C .
2 Peel fruit, remove all white pith; skewer peel onto wooden skewers, and place one in each bottle. Pour in warm vinegar, then seal. Shake occasionally.

83 BLUEBERRY VINEGAR
Makes about 8 cups (2 liters)

Ingredients
*6 cups (1.5 liters) cider
vinegar & 1 lemon
2lb (1kg) blueberries*
SHELF LIFE
2 years

GOOSEBERRY VINEGAR
*4 cups (150g) spinach and
2 pints (1kg) gooseberries
in place of the blueberries
makes a fine, pale vinegar.*

1 Bring the vinegar to a boil in a non-corrosive pan and boil rapidly for 1–2 minutes. Remove from the heat and allow to cool.
2 Scrub and peel the lemon and place the peel in a large jar.
3 Wash the blueberries and drain well. Coarsely chop the fruit in a food processor, and transfer to the jar with the lemon peel.
4 Pour the cooled vinegar into the jar, then cover with a clean cloth and leave in a warm, not hot, place for 3–4 weeks, shaking the jar from time to time to blend the ingredients.
5 Strain liquid and fruit through a jelly bag (*Tip 33*), then filter (*Tip 34*). Pour into sterilized bottles, then seal.
6 The vinegar may be cloudy at first, but the sediment should settle after a few weeks.

84 SUGAR-FREE SWEET VINEGAR

Makes about 4¾ quarts (4.3 liters)

Ingredients

*4½ quarts (4 liters) cider
(or distilled malt) vinegar
1⅓ cups (300ml) concentrated
apple or pear juice
2 tbsp each whole coriander
& peppercorns; 2 tsp cloves
1 tbsp whole allspice
3 cinnamon sticks*

SHELF LIFE
Indefinite

1 Put the vinegar and fruit juice in a non-corrosive pan. Bring to a boil and skim the liquid well.

2 Make a spice bag with the remaining ingredients (*Tip 35*). Add a few fresh or dried chilies to the bag if you wish. Place the bag in the boiling vinegar and boil for 10 minutes.

3 Remove the spice bag. Pour the vinegar into hot, sterilized bottles, then seal.

4 The vinegar is ready to use immediately, but improves with keeping.

85 STRAWBERRY VINEGAR

Makes about 2 quarts (2 liters)

Ingredients

*5 cups (1.25 liters) cider
(or white wine) vinegar
2 pints (1kg) full-flavored,
ripe strawberries
A few basil leaves
& wild strawberries
(both optional)*

SHELF LIFE
2 years

1 Boil vinegar rapidly in a non-corrosive pan for 1–2 minutes. Remove from heat; cool to 104°F/40°C.

2 Hull, chop strawberries. Place in a large glass bowl; pour in vinegar; mix well. Cover with a clean cloth and allow to stand for 2 weeks.

3 Strain liquid through a jelly bag (*Tip 33*); filter (*Tip 34*). Pour into sterilized bottles. Skewer basil leaves and strawberries, if using, and add to each bottle. Seal.

86 CLARIFYING VINEGAR

If the vinegar is cloudy, leave it in a cool, dark place to settle the sediment, then siphon off the clear liquid. If it is still cloudy, clarify it by beating 2 egg whites with a little of the vinegar until frothy. Add this to the bottle and shake. Allow to settle, then siphon off the vinegar.

PICKLES & SAUCES

87 PICKLED PLUMS
Makes about 2lb (1kg)

Ingredients
2 cups (500ml) cider vinegar
⅔ cup (150ml) concentrated apple or pear juice
1 tbsp salt
2lb (1kg) prune plums
8 cloves
8 whole allspice
6–8 strands finely shredded ginger root
2 bay leaves

SHELF LIFE
2 years

1 Put the cider vinegar, fruit juice, and salt in a non-corrosive pan. Bring to a boil and boil for 1–2 minutes.
2 Prick the plums all over with a wooden cocktail stick and arrange in hot, sterilized jars with the spices and bay leaves.
3 Add the boiling vinegar to cover the fruit, then seal the jars.
4 The plums will be ready to eat in 1 month but improve with keeping.

THE RIGHT PLUM
The best plums to pickle are the small, dark Switzen plums. Other varieties, such as Stanley plums (shown top right), can be pickled, but avoid using over-ripe fruit.

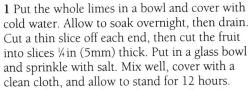
88 LIME PICKLE
Makes about 2lb (1kg)

Ingredients
2lb (1kg) limes
½ cup (100g) salt
6 whole cardamom pods
1 tsp each black cumin seeds & cumin seeds
½ tsp whole cloves
2 cups (500g) soft light brown or white sugar
1 tbsp powdered chili
2½oz (75g) fresh ginger root

SHELF LIFE
2 years

1 Put the whole limes in a bowl and cover with cold water. Allow to soak overnight, then drain. Cut a thin slice off each end, then cut the fruit into slices ¼in (5mm) thick. Put in a glass bowl and sprinkle with salt. Mix well, cover with a clean cloth, and allow to stand for 12 hours.

2 Next day, grind the cardamom and cumin to a powder in a spice mill or coffee grinder.

3 Drain the limes and put the liquid they have produced in a preserving pan with the sugar and ground spices. Bring to a boil, stirring until the sugar has dissolved, and boil for 1 minute. Remove from the heat, stir in the powdered chili, and allow to cool.

4 Finely shred the fresh ginger root and add with the limes to the cooled syrup. Mix well. Pack into sterilized jars. Gently prod the limes a few times with a wooden skewer to ensure there are no air pockets, then seal.

5 Leave in a warm (but not hot) place, such as a bright windowsill or shelf, for 4–5 days, and then store cool and dry. The pickle will be ready to eat in 4–5 weeks but improves with keeping.

SERVING SUGGESTIONS
This is a sharp, tangy, hot pickle from the Punjab in India. It can be served as a relish with a selection of appetizers, or spread over whole fish or fish filets before baking. The recipe can also be made with lemons, oranges, or other small citrus fruit.

89 SPICED WHOLE ORANGES

Makes about 2lb (1kg)

Ingredients

2lb (1kg) small, thin-skinned oranges
4 cups (1 liter) cider vinegar or distilled malt vinegar
3 cups (750g) sugar
Juice of 1 lemon
3 tsp whole cloves
2 cinnamon sticks & 1 tsp cardamom pods, crushed

SHELF LIFE
2 years

SPICE BAG FOR STEP 3
Make a spice bag of 2 tsp cloves, crushed cinnamon and cardamom, and removed orange peel.

1 Scrub oranges well; remove alternate strips of peel from each.
2 Put oranges in preserving pan; cover with cold water. Bring to a boil; simmer for 20–25 minutes until peel is just soft. Lift out oranges and drain well.
3 Measure 4 cups (1 liter) of the cooking liquid and return to pan. Add vinegar, lemon juice, and spice bag. Boil for 10 minutes, skim well, and add oranges; allow to stand overnight.
4 Next day, return mixture to boil, then simmer for 20 minutes. Remove oranges from liquid; allow to cool slightly.
5 Stud each orange with cloves and place in a sterilized jar. Boil syrup until it thickens slightly; pour into jar to cover oranges, then seal.

90 PRESERVED LEMONS

Makes about 2lb (1kg)

Ingredients

2lb (1kg) small, thin-skinned lemons
Salt (Step 1)
1½ cups (350ml) lemon or lime juice or acidulated water
1–2 tbsp olive oil

SHELF LIFE
2 years

1 Wash and scrub lemons. Slice into quarters lengthwise, leaving the sections attached at the stem. Sprinkle each section with 1 tsp salt.
2 Pack lemons tightly into a sterilized jar and weight down (*Tip 30*). Allow to stand in a warm, but not hot, place for 4–5 days.
3 Pour citrus juice or acidulated water (*Tip 25*) into the jar, covering the lemons.
4 Pour oil into top of jar in a thin layer and seal immediately. Keep for 3–4 weeks until the brine clears. The lemons are then ready to eat.

91 STRIPED SPICED PEARS
Makes about 2lb (1kg)

Ingredients
Juice of 1 lemon
2lb (1kg) hard pears
5 cups (1.25 liters) red wine vinegar
2 cups (500ml) red wine
2 cups (500g) sugar
1 cup (250g) honey
2 tsp whole cloves
1 tbsp black peppercorns
2 tsp whole allspice
1 tsp lavender flowers
(optional)
2 bay leaves
1 long cinnamon stick
Few strips lemon peel

SHELF LIFE
2 years

1 Stir lemon juice into a large bowl of cold water. Peel alternate strips of skin from the pears to form stripes, and place fruit in bowl.

2 Put vinegar, wine, sugar, and honey in a preserving pan.

3 Make a spice bag (*Tip 35*) with the cloves, peppercorns, whole allspice, lavender flowers, if using, bay leaves, cinnamon stick, and strips of lemon peel; add spice bag to pan. Bring to boil, skim well, and boil for 5 minutes.

4 Add pears, reduce heat, and simmer gently for 35–40 minutes until pears have softened slightly.

5 Lift pears out of pan with a slotted spoon and arrange in hot, sterilized jar.

6 Boil syrup rapidly until it is reduced by half and slightly thickened; remove spice bag.

7 Pour hot syrup in jar to cover pears, then seal. The pears will be ready to eat in 1 month.

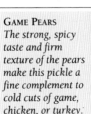

GAME PEARS
The strong, spicy taste and firm texture of the pears make this pickle a fine complement to cold cuts of game, chicken, or turkey.

92 CHINESE-STYLE PLUM SAUCE
Makes about 2 pints (1 liter)

Ingredients

*4lb (2kg) red plums, or 2lb
(1kg) each plums & damsons*
*4 cups (1 liter) red wine
(or rice) vinegar*
2 tsp salt
1 tbsp crushed star anise
2 tsp crushed Sichuan pepper
1 tsp crushed dried red chilies
*1 cup (250ml) dark
soy sauce*
*1 cup (300g) honey or
dark brown sugar*
*1 tbsp arrowroot or
cornstarch*
SHELF LIFE
2 years, heat-processed

1 Put the plums, vinegar, and salt into a preserving pan.
2 Make a spice bag (*Tip 35*) with the star anise, pepper, and chilies, and add to pan.
3 Bring to a boil, reduce the heat, and simmer for about 25 minutes, until plums are soft.
4 Discard the spice bag. Pass the plums through a sieve. Put the purée into the cleaned pan and stir in the soy sauce and honey or sugar. Bring to a boil, then simmer for 45 minutes, until the purée has reduced by one-quarter.
5 Mix the arrowroot to a paste with water. Stir into the pan and cook for 1–2 minutes, stirring well. Pour into hot, sterilized bottles, then seal. Heat-process (*Tip 24*), cool, check the seals, and dip corks in wax (*Tip 20*). The sauce is ready immediately, but improves with keeping.

93 DATE SAUCE
Makes about 2 pints (1 liter)

Ingredients

5oz (150g) tamarind block
*1½ cups (350ml) boiling
water*
2in (5cm) fresh ginger root
3–4 dried red chilies
1lb (500g) pitted dates
8 garlic cloves
*4 cups (1 liter) red wine
vinegar*
2 tsp salt
SHELF LIFE
2 years

1 Soak the tamarind in boiling water for 30 minutes. Strain, then pour liquid into preserving pan.
2 Peel and chop the ginger root, seed and chop the chilies, and chop the dates and garlic. Add to the pan with the vinegar and salt.
3 Bring to a boil, simmer for 10 minutes, then cool.
4 Purée in a food processor. Return to the cleaned pan and boil for 1–2 minutes. Pour into hot, sterilized bottles, then seal.

CHUTNEYS

94 GINGER CHUTNEY

Makes about 3 pints (1.5kg)

Ingredients
*10oz (300g) fresh ginger
root*
2 medium red peppers
1 large cucumber
2 large onions
4 lemons
1¼ cups (250g) raisins
*4 cups (1 liter) cider
(or white wine) vinegar*
*2 cups (500g) granulated
sugar*
2 tsp salt
SHELF LIFE
2 years

1 Shred ginger root; dice peppers; quarter cucumber lengthwise and then slice thickly; coarsely chop onions. Halve lemons lengthwise, removing seeds, and slice thinly.
2 Put these prepared ingredients with the raisins and vinegar into a preserving pan. Bring to a boil, then reduce the heat and simmer gently for about 30 minutes, until the lemon peel and vegetables have softened.
3 Add the sugar and salt to the pan, stirring until they have dissolved. Simmer for a further 30–45 minutes, until most of the liquid has evaporated and the chutney is thick.
4 Ladle the mixture into hot, sterilized jars, then seal. This chutney improves with keeping.

95 SUCCESSFUL CHUTNEYS

Use mellow vinegars for chutneys: cider, wine, or citrus vinegars are best, since malt vinegar produces too harsh a result. Keep chutneys for at least 1 month to allow time for their flavors to blend and mellow. The size of the ingredients determines the texture of the finished chutney: the smaller the pieces, the smoother the result.

96 PLUM CHUTNEY
Makes about 2 pints (1kg)

Ingredients
1lb (500g) dark red plums
1lb (500g) light plums
6 garlic cloves & 6 red chilies
⅓ cup (75ml) water
4oz (125g) tamarind block
3 cups (750ml) red wine vinegar
1½ cups (400g) light brown or white sugar
2 tsp salt & 1 tsp cloves
1 tsp whole allspice
1 broken cinnamon stick
½ tsp black cumin seeds

SHELF LIFE
2 years

1 Cut plums in half and remove pits. Crack pits with a nutcracker or a hammer and tie them in a piece of muslin.
2 Coarsely chop garlic cloves and fresh red chilies and place with plums, muslin bag, and water in preserving pan. Bring to a boil, then simmer gently, stirring frequently, for 15–20 minutes or until the plums are soft.
3 Soak tamarind block in ½ cup (125ml) hot water for 20 minutes, then sieve out and discard any large seeds. Alternatively, use 2 tbsp tamarind paste.
4 Add vinegar, sieved tamarind or paste, sugar, and salt to the pan. Bring to a boil, stirring until they have dissolved. Simmer for 25–30 minutes, stirring frequently, until most of the liquid has evaporated and the mixture is thick. Remove from the heat and take out the muslin bag.
5 Grind cloves, whole allspice, and cinnamon stick to a powder in a spice mill or coffee grinder. Stir into the mixture with the black cumin seeds.
6 Ladle the chutney into hot, sterilized jars, then seal. The chutney will be ready to eat in 1 month.

CHOICE PLUMS
Select firm, fleshy plums with a good color for this chutney. A mixture of light and dark red plums is ideal, but any single kind of plums or any combination will do as well.

97 APPLE CHUTNEY
Makes about 4 pints (2kg)

Ingredients
2½lb (1.25kg) under-ripe
cooking apples
1¼lb (625g) onions
2 lemons
2 garlic cloves (optional)
2 cups (300g) raisins
2 cups (500ml) cider
vinegar
2 cups (400g) dark brown
sugar & 1 tbsp salt
1 tsp each of ground ginger,
cinnamon, & turmeric
SHELF LIFE
1 year

1 Peel, core, and coarsely chop apples; peel and coarsely chop onions; finely slice lemons into semi-circles; finely chop garlic cloves, if using.
2 Put apples, onions, lemons, garlic, raisins, and cider vinegar in a preserving pan. Bring to a boil, then simmer for 15–20 minutes until the apples soften but still retain some texture.
3 Add sugar, stirring until it has dissolved. Simmer for 30–45 minutes, until most of the liquid has evaporated and the mixture is thick. Remove from the heat; add salt and the three ground spices.
4 Ladle into hot, sterilized jars, then seal. The chutney will be ready to eat in 1 month.

98 PEACH CHUTNEY
Makes about 3½ pints (1.75kg)

Ingredients
2lb (1kg) peaches
2 medium cooking apples
2 lemons & 3 garlic cloves
2½oz (75g) ginger root
½lb (275g) shallots
½lb (250g) seedless grapes
2 cups (500ml) cider
vinegar; 1 cup (250g) sugar
1 tsp whole cloves
6 cardamom pods
2in (5cm) cinnamon stick
2 tsp caraway seeds
SHELF LIFE
6 months

1 Skin, pit, and slice peaches; peel, core, and chop apples; slice lemons; shred garlic and ginger root; chop shallots.
2 Place ingredients with grapes and vinegar in a preserving pan. Bring to a boil, then reduce heat and simmer for 25 minutes until apples are soft.
3 Add sugar, stirring until dissolved. Simmer for 35–40 minutes until most of liquid has evaporated and mixture is thick. Remove from heat.
4 Grind spices to a powder; sieve into chutney. Add caraway seeds and mix well. Ladle mixture into sterilized jars, then seal. Eat after 1 month.

99 HOT MANGO CHUTNEY
Makes about 3 pints (1.5kg)

Ingredients

4lb (2kg) unripe mangoes
2 lemons or limes
3–4 fresh red chilies
3 cups (750ml) white wine
(or distilled white) vinegar
2 cups (500g) light brown
sugar & 1 tbsp salt
1 tbsp green cardamom
pods & 1 tsp cumin seeds
1 tsp powdered chili
(optional) & 1 tsp turmeric
SHELF LIFE
2 years

1 Peel, pit, and cut mangoes into chunks; slice lemons or limes; seed and coarsely chop chilies. Place in preserving pan with vinegar.
2 Bring to a boil, reduce the heat, then simmer for 10–15 minutes until mango is just tender. Add sugar and salt, stirring until dissolved. Simmer for 50–60 minutes, until most of the liquid has evaporated.
3 Grind green cardamom and cumin. Sieve with powdered chili into chutney; add turmeric. Ladle into hot, sterilized jars; seal.

100 EXOTIC FRUIT CHUTNEY
Makes about 6 pints (3kg)

Ingredients

1 small pineapple
1lb (500g) apples
1¼ cups (300g) dried apricots
½lb (250g) baby corn
½lb (250g) kumquats
4 cups (1 liter) cider (or
white wine) vinegar
3–4 fresh red chilies
2 cups (500g) sugar
2 tbsp black mustard seeds
2 tbsp salt
1 tbsp green peppercorns
1 bunch chopped mint
SHELF LIFE
1 year

1 Peel, core, and chop pineapple into chunks; peel, core, and chop apples; soak and chop apricots; quarter baby corn lengthwise. Use sliced oranges if kumquats are unavailable.
2 Put all fruit in a preserving pan with the corn and vinegar. Bring to a boil, then simmer for 15 minutes.
3 Seed and chop chilies. Add to pan with sugar, mustard seeds, salt, and peppercorns. Stir until the sugar has dissolved. Simmer, stirring frequently, for 50–60 minutes, until most of the liquid has evaporated and the mixture is thick.
4 Remove from the heat; stir in the mint. Ladle into hot, sterilized jars, then seal. The chutney is ready in 1 month, but improves with age.

101 FIG CHUTNEY

Makes about 4 pints (2kg)

Ingredients

*5 cups (1.25 liters) red
wine vinegar
2 cups (500g) light
brown sugar
2 tbsp salt
2lb (1kg) slightly
under-ripe black figs
1lb (500g) onions
½lb (250g) pitted dates
5oz (150g) fresh ginger root
2 tbsp sweet paprika
1 tbsp white mustard seeds
3 tbsp fresh or 1 tbsp
dried tarragon*

SHELF LIFE
1 year

1 Put the vinegar, sugar, and salt into a preserving pan, stirring until the sugar and salt have dissolved. Bring to a boil, then simmer for about 5 minutes.

2 Slice figs and onions; coarsely chop dates; finely shred ginger root. Add to the pan with the paprika and mustard seeds, bring to a boil, then simmer for 1 hour.

3 Remove from the heat, add the tarragon; mix well. Ladle into hot, sterilized jars; seal. The chutney will be ready in 1 month.

STORING HERBS
*Keep herbs fresh in
a jar of water, or put in
the refrigerator with the
stems wrapped in damp
paper towels. Since dried
herbs may taste stronger
than fresh, substitute half
the amount if need be.*

INDEX

ACKNOWLEDGMENTS

Dorling Kindersley would like to thank Hilary Bird for compiling the index, Richard Hammond for proofreading, and Mark Bracey and Robert Campbell for DTP assistance.

Author's Appreciation
I would like to thank Saul Radomsky for his patience and support, and the many friends who have helped, schlepped, tasted, and commented: Trudy Barnham, the Blacher family, Jon, Ann, and Marjorie Bryent, Iris & John Cole, the Hersch family, Jill Jago, Dalia Lamdani, Joy Peacock, Bob and Ann Tilley, Eric Treuille, and Jo Wightman. Finally, many thanks to Alison Austin, who assisted me with the food styling, and Vicky McIver, my agent.

Photography
All photographs by Ian O'Leary, assisted by Emma Brogi.